Homesteading For Beginners

How to Build a Profitable Homestead Backyard Farm and Make Money from Urban Farming the Easy Way: A Self-Sufficiency Survival Guide for the Urban Farmer and Prepping Enthusiasts

By William Walsworth

Table of Contents

Introduction

With more and more people choosing technology over spending time in nature, the many stressful situations of the fast-paced life have taken over much of our current modern society. As an opposing force to this modernized stressed life, more people find the appeal and joy in going back to their natural roots. It comes to no surprise that more and more people are choosing to take the slow and sustainable lifestyle over the busy, fast-paced city life. One of the movements that has sprouted from this is the growing group of people seeking to go back to nature: growing their own foods on their own lands, in their own organic and sustainable way. Homesteading is one of the key ways to allow the urban and suburban population go back to its natural roots and get their hands green again.

Living and working on a homestead is as much an occupational journey as it is a personal one. Becoming a homestead entrepreneur will allow you to learn and grow as a person as you work hard to see your business grow. Like most things in life, it won't always be an easy journey, but the potential benefits are also limitless. While managing your own homestead, you'll be able to provide for yourself and your family while also remaining self-sufficient in how you create your stream(s) of income. Being self-sufficient and being able to live on your own terms is a hard-earned rewards in and of themselves. Not everyone has the capacity to fulfill their dreams in a similar fashion. Another great benefit you will be able to enjoy, are the benefits of food security and locally grown fresh fruits and vegetables, as well as a multitude of other great farmer's products. These products will not only save you a lot of money on groceries, but they allow you to discover new tastes, put you on track towards a healthier diet and are also of great education to children. Not once will your child tell you that milk comes from the supermarket, when you bring home some fresh bottles from your cattle.

In today's economy, the only real job security is a job that you can create for yourself. Traditional farms on the decline, many people living in both the urban and suburban areas are becoming homestead entrepreneurs by using their own skills, knowledge and their own land to make them a hefty income on the side.

Whether you're considering homesteading part-time or becoming completely self-sufficient as a full-time homesteader, there are many tips and tricks to living off of your own land that you'll need to know in order to prosper on the homestead. You'll have to wear a variety of different hats on a daily basis in order to make it as a successful homestead entrepreneur.

In this book, we'll show you how homesteading can become one of the most lucrative professions of the 21st century. You will also be explained why now is the best time to become a homestead entrepreneur. We'll briefly go over the history of homesteading and take a look at how the profession grew out of necessity and into opportunity. We'll also show you how to lay out a basic plan for building your local homestead operation and how to carve out a successful business living off of your own land. We'll talk about the basics of business, including how to file for a business license and what other certification is required of most homesteads today. You'll learn about all of the different cash crops that homestead entrepreneurs use to maximize the amount of money they make per square inch of land they own, including some of the most popular cash crops in today's market. Furthermore, the market value for different types of crops will be considered. We'll also show you some very interesting and lucrative ways that a homestead entrepreneur can make money in today's market, simply by living off of your own land. We'll show you some of the secrets that successful homestead entrepreneurs are applying to keep everything running just the way it's supposed to. We'll also show you some common mistakes made by first time homesteaders and how you can avoid them. Lastly, we'll show you how to take your homestead business even further by buying more property, adding other money makers to your property, and expanding your local homestead operation.

Get ready for the first major investment in your future homestead business: learning about all of the essentials. In this introductory book we'll talk about plenty of different resources that are essential to building a successful homestead business. But above all, the most valuable resource that any homestead entrepreneur can invest in is their own time, skills and knowledge. The success you will have will be equal to or even bigger than the effort you will put into this. As long as you approach your homestead as a business, you find yourself in the correct mindset to be able to grow and prosper from your own backyard. First, we will go over an essential but necessary question: why would we even begin this homestead operation? This is a question we ask ourselves not to check if we have gone mental, but to reaffirm the reasons as to why homesteading is a great sustainable business idea.

Why Would One Choose Homesteading?

There are many valid reasons why people would consider homesteading. Whether you live in amid skyscrapers or soccer moms, in an apartment or tact home, the benefits of homesteading are the same. By growing your own food, you will be able to achieve self-sufficiency, better nutrition for you and your family, extra income and business insights, you will be closer to nature, and you will even own your own business and could consider calling yourself a CEO. "William Walsworth, CEO of Homestead Farms Inc." Sounds pretty nifty, right?

All silliness aside, producing food is a great way to help other people. No matter where you live, food remains to be an invaluable resource. The number of traditional, full-time farmers is dwindling and many communities now turn to homesteaders for their produce. In fact, according to the US Department of Agriculture, the number of farms in the US has dropped by half in the last decade alone. It's not surprising, then, that homesteads are growing faster than weeds, and they're breaking all of the rules of traditional farming. Probably anyone would choose to have eggs from a local homestead farm, instead of having to buy eggs that where processed in a giant factory. Local, organic and sustainable is hot, that is an undeniable fact of today's society.

Another great consideration, is that you don't need a hundred acres or even a dozen acres to be a successful homesteader. The whole idea of homesteading revolves around the concept of using a relatively small piece of land to efficiently produce hand-made and locally grown farmer's products. Most produce that is coming from a homestead has been grown on as little as half an acre, or sometimes even less. The best part is, that locally grown produce is always in high demand. Generally, your most loyal customers don't even live more than a stone's throw away from your homestead. This simple fact greatly enhances the quality and value of the products you will be going to sell to the local community.

We could really say that the stereotypical reclusive, rural farmer is a thing of the past. Some of the most successful homesteaders are part-timers, such as the lawyer that grows gourmet garlic in his spare time just to relieve stress, the retired teacher who earns most of her retirement income by farming bamboo, and the home designer who makes a killing in the local market with the mushrooms she grows in the shed in the backyard while looking after her three kids.

For some, homesteading is a passion. They do it just for a sense of satisfaction, when they go to bed at night knowing that they were able to produce something that is natural and delicious. For most people, however, it is generally about the financial profit and the freedom you have of making your source of income on your own piece of farmer's land. Whatever side you choose, I like to take the middle route. Why not live a great homesteading life on your own terms, produce value to the community with your products, and allow yourself to become a little richer from it? There is no shame in benefiting from something that provides so much joy to others. To me, it really is the combination of considerations that makes homesteading such a great opportunity for anyone to get into. And yes it takes knowledge and effort, but the rewards are invaluable and you will teach yourself so much along the process. Even the learning process alone is a valuable consideration to take into account. Even when you fail to become profitable in the long run, the things you will learn will stick with you for a lifetime. Anyone infected with that entrepreneurial bug will change their mindset and become a different and improved person because of it. So why not at least try?

A Brief History of Homesteading

Before we delve into the specifics of how you can sow seeds and reap dollars right in your own backyard, it is important to first understand how homesteading came to be as it exists today. The most valuable resource to any homestead entrepreneur is information. By taking a look at some of the earliest homestead entrepreneurs, we'll get an idea of what makes a successful homestead. A brief glance into the past also provides some great inspiration to the possibilities of starting your own homestead farm. Learning from the founders of modern homesteading is like taking an inside look into the essence of why anyone would go about creating their own homestead operation. So let's jump into the past and look at what our trusty old folks, our ancestors, did to cultivate their own plots of land and grow some great products on it.

Going way back...

Dating all the way back to ancient Egypt, the waste of the community was used by common folk to start homesteads. In Machu Picchu, the stepped architecture made it easy for water to be conserved and reused, creating rich vegetable beds at the base of the community's structures. It wasn't until the 19th century that a more urbanized version of homesteading started to develop in Germany. As a response to the food scarcity and poverty, urban residents created allotment gardens as a way to help feed other members of the community. During WWI and WWII, the US, Canada and the UK started Victory Gardens to reduce the pressure of massive amounts of food production going on to support the war efforts abroad.

During the great depression, community gardening became very popular and provided low income neighborhoods with an abundance of fresh fruit and vegetables as well as providing citizens with a space to cultivate plants of their own. It was during this time when became scare for communities that the idea of investing in food security became popular. People wanted an alternative from the supplemental food produced in rural farms and distant imports, as they were not sustainable.

War and depression: what an opportunity!

As early as 1893, citizens of a depression-struck Detroit were asked to use any vacant lots to grow vegetables. They were nicknamed Pingree's Potato Patches after the mayor, Hazen S. Pingree, who came up with the idea. He intended for these gardens to produce income, food supply, and even boost independence during times of hardship.

During the First World War, President Woodrow Wilson called upon all American citizens to utilize any available open space for food growth, seeing this as a way to pull them out of a potentially damaging situation. Because most of Europe was consumed with war, they were unable to produce sufficient food supplies to be shipped to the U.S., and a new plan was implemented with the intent to feed the U.S. and even supply a surplus to other countries in need. By the year 1919, over 5 million plots were growing food and over 500 million pounds of produce was harvested.

A very similar practice came into use during the Great Depression that provided a purpose, a job, and food to those who would otherwise be without anything during such harsh times. In this case, these efforts helped to raise spirits socially as well as to boost economic growth. Over 2.8 million dollars' worth of food was produced from the subsistence gardens during the Depression.

By the time of the Second World War, the War/Food Administration set up a National Victory Garden Program that set out to systematically establish functioning agriculture within cities. With this new plan in action, as many as 5.5 million Americans took part in the victory garden movement and over 9 million pounds of fruit and vegetables were grown a year, accounting for 44% of U.S.-grown produce throughout that time.

Modern times, modern needs

Today, even the biggest cities around the world who have no threat of a food shortage anytime soon are encouraged to grow their own food. In 2010, New York City saw the building and opening of the world's largest privately owned and operated rooftop farm, followed by an even larger location in 2012. Both were a result of municipal programs such as The

Green Roof Tax Abatement Program and Green Infrastructure Grant Program.

Because of the advent of modern agriculture technology, urban farming is practical for both developing countries and developed countries. Because access to nutritious food is not always easy for all populations, both economically and geographically, there is a push in recent years for communities, especially large cities, to become self-sufficient. Many of these cities actively encourage the urban farming movement under the umbrella of sustainable policies, which in turn benefited the movement that sprouted many of these urban homesteads around the cities.

Cities who are faced with food shortages have very limited options: to eat whatever form of sustenance is attainable or starve. While history tells us that communities who are in short supply of food rarely starve, there are a myriad of dangerous health-related problems that arise in people who are forced to live on a low calorie diet.

Historically, urban agriculture policies have been tied of a number of documented social benefits, including citizens reporting an overall improvement in emotional well-being, documented improved health, increased income, a higher employment rate, improved social relationships, increased community pride, social well-being within the community even lower crime and suicide rates. Individuals who take part in community gardens also report better mental health, decreased stress and feeling more calm and relaxed when they have the opportunity to work in the community garden with their neighbors.

Although agriculture has always been one of the foundations upon which the human race has thrived, the concept of urban homesteading for money is a fairly new concept in our modernized societies. With the rapid rise of the world's population, the need for fresh and safe produce is never ending. While most people in the first world countries have no problem gathering their foods from the store, they too prefer local produce over mass-produced crops.

There is a reason that organic, green and local are buzzwords in food marketing these days – the consumer is seeking to get back in touch with their needs and to reconnect with the land and nature itself. People would much rather pay for food that is locally sourced rather than imported from half a world away and loaded with preservatives. For all of these reasons and more, now is the best time to become a homestead entrepreneur.

The Basics – Towards an Action Plan

In this section, we'll cover all of the essential tools you'll need to start your own homestead, what types of skills are required to get the most out of your crops, how to get the most money per square inch of land and an action plan for jumpstarting your own homestead.

Since every homestead is unique, the first thing you need to do is determine what the objective is with your farm and what your specific needs are. Grab a pen and paper and prepare to make your pre-farm checklist. Then allow yourself some time to think about the resources you need to attain those objectives. This entails financial investments, practical tools, but also knowledge of how to put it all together. When you have your resources list ready, it is time to transform your long-term objectives into milestones, which are the concrete smaller goals you have towards your business. This will eventually be molded into an overall action plan, which is the things you will do to achieve those milestones (and eventually your objectives). Writing out your plan for your own homestead situation will make things much easier on you in the long run and allow you to keep some oversight into the objectives you have set.

Objective

The first thing you want to uncover for yourself is what your end-goals are with your homesteading business. Before you begin your homesteading journey, it's very important that you ask yourself what you hope to accomplish by growing your own food. When you have a clearly definite objective in mind, finding a way to get there will be much easier. It is recommendable to both set an income goal and a goal regarding the size and diversity of the products you deliver. You could also set goals regarding overall product quality and quantity, the degree to which you want to be scaling up your business or other homestead-related objectives. It all depends on what you personally want to get out of this business.

Do you simply want to save money by growing your own nutritious food for your family, or do you want to turn your land into a money making machine and provide great farmer's products to the community?

Maybe a little bit of both? Do you plan to focus entirely on cash crops (those crops that will efficiently make you the most amount of revenue), sell everything to the community and then buy all of your food at the local grocery store, or will you dedicate a portion of your land to crops that you plan on consuming yourself? By the time you get started, you should already know how you're going to allocate your land. Maybe you will even dedicate portions of your land for other purposes than farming. As you will learn later on in this book, there are many more ways you can use your land and allow yourself to make money with your homestead operation. Thinking outside of the box is what will differentiate your business from others, and this is what will allow you to expand your business objectives beyond traditional means. Whatever yours is, write it down and never forget why you're doing this.

Resources

Now take note of all of the resources you have access to that will bring you closer to your objective. This includes any outdoor land, indoor spaces that can be utilized to grow, people power or extra helpers, any gardening tools you own or that you will regularly have access to such as shovels, shades, buckets, lighting equipment if you're growing indoors as well as extra soil, seeds, other gardening tools and so forth.

Also consider the resources you will need in order to turn your operation into a homesteading business. Depending on the products you will produce, these can differ greatly.

For the department of herbs, flowers, fruits and vegetables, you will need quality seeds, soil and perhaps even a greenhouse to grow your produce in throughout the seasons. You will need basic tools to work the land. You will also require herbicides, pesticides and protection from birds, foxes and other animals that might come and nibble on your delicious foods. If you are looking to work organically, which is highly recommendable for the quality of your final product, you might need some natural protection against this. Some ladybugs that will kill off those pesky insects, or some net constructions to ward of curious crows and hedgehogs.

Working with greenhouses might be a big initial investment, but it can help with both your produce protection and its continued growth. You can also more easily use your limited space by familiarizing yourself with vertical gardening constructions.

On the other hand, using the open space of your land will allow you to more easily pollinate your crops and cross-breed them if needed. Let's say you are keeping bees: wouldn't it be great to use your bee army to pollinate your own crops? The circle of nature can be of great use. Even free-roaming groups of chickens might help with picking out some wheat, unwanted insects or spiders, and keeping the soil alive by stirring it up in a natural way. Using your resources in combination can not only mimic the natural situation more accurately, but will also allow you to decrease your required efforts on the land itself. Setting up a small ecosystem this way will allow you to greatly increase your small-scale natural production site.

In the administrative department, you want to keep track of your financial resources as well. How much money are you willing to invest into your business? Will you be able to build that chicken pen or that goat shelter? Is there enough investment available for packaging and transportation? Know your investment capacities, as well as your ability and willingness to ask the bank for a loan. Make sure that in the long-term your operation becomes profitable and have a plan set up on how to achieve that. Without a long-term exit strategy your business will likely fail and you are likely to go bankrupt. So please work out your finances with the help of an expert if needed. And you also want some legal insurance for the people that work on your farm or are visitors: you will not want to be liable for any possible injuries while people are on your land.

Milestones

Next, come up with a list of smaller goals leading up to your main objective and a realistic timeline to achieve these. This is a good way to measure your progress. For example, your first milestone might be to make $200 in the next month just from selling the food that you grow. This will vary depending on the amount of resources you currently have.

The milestones are best set according to the specific months you are working in. And those can be broken down into weekly goals if you desire so. With the milestones, you must certainly take into account the seasonal variations. You don't need to be a farmer to know that some months are more profitable when it comes to harvest time than others. You must be able to deal with these variations in income and account for them pre-emptively.

The milestones you set are best differentiated into the different products you (plan to) sell or use. This way you will also learn what part of your operation is most profitable and what the income variations are per time period. It is very clever to set aside parts of your revenue for investment into new part of your homestead. Building constructions or buying large tools are the biggest investments to consider here. You can incorporate these goals into your milestones and set some of your future milestones to buy or install some of these elements onto your land.

If you feel like the administrative part of your business is too complicated and you wish to focus mainly on being on your land, this is completely understandable. You can easily hire a professional for a low cost to do these administrative tasks for you in the blink of an eye. You can consult your local financial expert to help you get in touch with a professional to help you with these tasks quickly.

Plan

Here is where the fun part begins, for me at least. Using the resources you listed above, come up with a way to achieve your first milestone. On a separate list, write down all of resources that your do not have which will crucial to completing your first milestone. This will be your shopping list.

At each milestone you can revisit your list, or make a new one, and see how close you are to accomplishing your main objective. Don't worry if you get stuck on any part of this list. This book will help you hammer out all of the little details along the way. Always remember that your number one resource while homesteading will be your own resourcefulness and ability to adapt to new situations. Effectively applying this creative ability is how some homestead entrepreneurs have allowed themselves to scale their operation towards making six-figure incomes, simply by living off of their own land.

After taking stock of your land, start researching what you want to plant. When choosing what to grow in your homestead, making the best use out of every square inch of land is the name of the game. While you are taking stock of your land, ask yourself: What plants or other farmer's products are popular on the market every year? Is there enough demand to support profitable prices? Is it reasonably easy to grow or produce? Can it be grown in my own soil or within the limits of my land? What special needs will each plant or product require? Do I have the skills, people power and resources necessary to grow these plants or products? Will I be able to earn a decent income with this plant or product given the land that I have?

The most important factors to consider when choosing what to grow on your land when it comes to herbs, flowers, fruits and vegetables should be:

1. The market value of a single crop when sold locally;
2. How much space a single crop will take up;
3. How much time it takes between sowing each crop to full maturity.

Now take the square footage of land that you will dedicate to your homestead and divide that by the amount of space that each individual crop will take up. Multiple that number by the market value for each crop when sold in your local market. That is the maximum amount of money you will be able to make from one harvest season. If you don't find that amount attractive enough to jump into sowing your crops, move on to another type of produce. By repeating this process, you will be able to uncover what works best for your land and find which products you are most comfortable producing. Maybe you even would limit yourself to chicken or goat-related products if that is most attractive to you. Every situation is different and the profitability is completely dependent on your profit calculations and preferences.

With the product revenue calculation, also take into account the possibility that a harvest can fail (either partially or completely). It is essential to diversity your income in order to reduce the risk of losing your income stream from your homestead operation. Therefore always consider to at least starting off with several types of products and not start a monoculture. The small-scale business operation compared to the traditional farmer's monoculture structure does not allow you to remain profitable if something goes wrong during the growth cycle of your products.

Finding your Cash Crops

When choosing your cash crop, which is the product or are the products you will be earning your income with over the long term, it is important to take into consideration the local market value. Before you even sow a single seed, ask yourself if you can make a living selling the crop of your choice in the local market. Crunching the numbers and finding potential buyers ahead of time will save you a world of headaches and frustration and allows you to effective plan out which direction you want to take your homestead operation.

Among your potential customers should be local restaurants, cafes, and bistros, as well as your own booth at your local farmer's market. While you may be able to make a couple of hundred bucks selling your crops at the farmer's market, local restaurants will be your bread and butter. These are the locations that are willing to pay you relatively large amounts of money for locally produced fresh products. Start by calling around to any non-franchise restaurants in your area and asking them where they get their produce from and if they would be interested in placing weekly orders of locally grown food. Once you are able to lock in a few weekly orders, your homesteading business is off and running before you've even planted your first crop.

Each local market will have different prices for different types of products, but let's take a look at an example of four types of high value cash crops. Some of these products might seem exotic, but they are carefully selected and generally have a high-profit margin. Looking into these products will certainly allow you to differentiate your operation from many other homesteaders in your local area, as most of them are not regularly produced by homesteaders or local farmers. While these four cash crops serve as an example, some research will allow you to think outside of the box enough to find the perfect product that will allow you to connect well with local businesses around you and find your first clients. So let's get into four example cash crops that you could consider getting into.

Bamboo

For thousands of years, bamboo has been an everyday part of Asian life, providing food, shelter and raw material for everything from garden fences to flutes. Several varieties of bamboo are grown just for their edible shoots, producing an edible harvest of up to ten tons per acre. Clearly, the multipurpose nature of this crop allows for a diversified market and creates many opportunities when it comes to selling the final product. With some basic knowledge of this crop you can easily come up with several uses for bamboo. And these uses are certainly not limited to the Asian market alone.

In North America and Europe, bamboo is being rediscovered as an essential landscaping plant and most Western-based bamboo growers cannot keep up with the demand. Bamboo is not just a tropical plant either – many varieties are grown in Japan and China, where the climate can be just as harsh as our northern states and provinces. One could easily found suitable soil and climate conditions for this crop to thrive on.

Landscapers of both private and public spaces are also using more and more bamboo instead of traditional shrubs. The high sustainable nature of the crop in combination with its relatively low cost allows bamboo to be a great tool in any landscaping project.

One could use bamboo as a hedge, a screen, as a specimen plant or as a shade plant. Bamboo keeps its green color through the winter, and it's easy to grow. Plus, you can get a big plant quickly, unlike trees that take years to mature. Potted bamboo plants can bring as much as $150 USD each in retail stores, and value-added bamboo products, such as fencing and garden art, will bring in even more. So it is certainly worth to consider to take your basic bamboo product and add value to it before selling it to retail stores or other market destinations.

Never forget about the market for transplanting and selling fully grown plants as well. Whether it is ginseng roots or whole fruit trees, some people will pay top dollar for a fully grown, healthy plant. This is a technique that can be applied not only to bamboo, but to most of your cash crops. While selling fully grown plants to the market does cost more time in terms of growth and caretaking, the value added because of this will certainly be worth the additional effort. The technique of growing out your crops to become full-sized is especially great if you are in the niche of specific garden plants or flowers. While some of these crops are more advanced in nature, the potential for such crops are immense and could really help your homestead to become increasingly profitable over the long haul.

Garlic

Garlic is a member of the same plant family as onions, shallots, leeks and chives. For thousands of years, garlic has been used for both cooking and medicinal purposes. Recent scientific research has proven many of the historical claims for garlic's healing powers. Its chemical ingredients can fight bacteria, lower cholesterol levels and act as an organic insecticide. Herbal remedies are a great option for homesteaders to get into. You do not require medical licenses to create healthy supplements. Private labelling your garlic medicine will allow you to penetrate both the medicinal and cosmetic markets for garlic-related produce. This can also be expanded to other types of medicinal or cosmetic herbal crops. The demand for these alternative and locally produced product has grown dramatically over the past decades and there is some interesting value to attain in this non-food niche as well.

The multi-purpose nature of the crop makes garlic an ideal crop for the relatively small grower who has limited experience and space, as it is almost foolproof to grow. Because it tolerates a wide variety of soils and weather, it's very hard to lose a crop. Even myself I have rarely been able to lose a garlic crop, and I live in the rainy parts of England. So surely you can outdo me without much trouble! The sturdy nature of the garlic plant is remarkable and makes the crop an ideal starter product. For decades, growers have nicknamed garlic "the mortgage lifter" for that very reason. Most homestead entrepreneurs fetch a higher price for their garlic by selling it in the form of garlic braids, fresh garlic greens and garlic powder. Your imagination in combination with the market demand is your only limitation here...

Ginseng

Once called "Green Gold" by farmers, ginseng is an ordinary looking plant that grows on the shaded forest floor. Its value lies in its slowly growing root. The Chinese have valued the ginseng root for thousands of years as the most potent of herbs and as a regenerative tonic. Since it was discovered in the

U.S. almost 300 years ago, most ginseng has been exported to Asia.

Although it takes 6 years before the slow growing ginseng roots are ready to harvest for market, most growers sell seed and two-year rootlets to earn an income from their ginseng crop in the years before the harvest. At current ginseng prices, a half-acre ginseng patch could produce $100,000 worth of seeds, rootlets and mature roots over that 6-year period, or over $16,000 per year. This is why ginseng is one of the most grown crops by homestead entrepreneurs. However, please take into account that ginseng really is a long-term herb that requires time to mature. Anyone seeking to get a quick return on their buck will not be wanting to get into ginseng immediately. It is like any good wine: with time comes quality. And in our case, with time comes quality and a crazy profitable ginseng harvest.

Oyster Mushrooms

Many homesteaders sell their entire crop at the Farmer's Market, where regular customers line up to buy the freshly harvested mushrooms every week.

Most mushrooms can be grown in a shed or barn with nothing more than a 40-watt light bulb. Many homesteaders are fond of these oyster mushrooms, because they are some of the easier to grow while still selling at a high price. You can obtain mushroom spawn with straw and put the straw in plastic bags with slits. A few weeks later, your mushroom crops will be ready to go. Quick and easy, just the way most people like it. Once you familiarize yourself with the basics of growing these mushrooms, you will have a great first cash crop for your farm. And you can easily grow these in the more shady areas of your homestead as well, which makes this crop so extraordinary. Set up a simple vertical gardening container, full them with mushroom spawn including the straw, install your light bulbs, and you're good to go. Keep the soil moist and your mushrooms will be right happy where they are.

In most areas, it's hard to find gourmet mushrooms that are locally grown, such as oyster and shiitake. Both have a short shelf life and do not stand up well to long distance shipping, which is why large mushroom producing companies won't even bother shipping their products to certain parts of the world. This is just one example where homesteaders have the advantage of producing local delicacies: large demand and few local sellers to fill in this demand. And there are many types of benefits to think of when you're attempting to market these products to people who are unfamiliar with these types of mushrooms. Gourmet mushrooms are fat-free, cholesterol free, pesticide free, have many medicinal benefits and gourmet mushrooms can be grown without any type of harmful chemicals.

Oyster mushrooms are ready to harvest in just six weeks, giving new homesteaders a fast payback on their investment, as well as the flexibility to increase production on the fly, in order to meet additional demand. Oyster mushrooms also produce heavy yields, too. The average is one pound of mushrooms for each pound of straw used to grow them. Most homesteaders can grow up to six batches of oyster mushrooms each year, allowing them to produce lots of mushrooms in a small space. A two hundred square foot growing area, for example, can produce up to as much as 5,000 to 6,000 pounds of mushrooms each year. In 2016, prices range from a wholesale price of $3 per pound up to $9 per pound when selling direct to the consumer, such as restaurants or at the farmer's market. Prices will vary from region to region, but in general, the fresh local mushrooms always bring top dollar on the local markets.

Now let's look at some other potential cash crops to help you bring your homestead to a state where it is highly profitable. Always keep asking yourself what homestead-related items people need and re willing buy on a regular basis. You may be surprised that people are willing to pay a few extra dollars to buy items that are locally grown, as opposed to the mass-produced stuff you find on grocery store shelves. And this demand goes far beyond herbs, flowers, fruits and vegetables. Let us take a brief look at some other possibilities.

Livestock

If you have a surplus of land, you may want to consider raising some livestock. Again, be sure to check your local agriculture laws before investing in any livestock, but consider the long-term revenue that chickens and cows can produce, for example. People always want farm-fresh eggs, and having even one or two cows or goats on hand will allow you to produce and sell your own milk. Once you start producing your own milk, you will also be able to sell your own cheese in the market – another high value item, especially if it's produced locally!

Although items like eggs, cheese and milk will be your top dollar products when you own livestock, you can also make quite a bit of money by selling meat, breeding and selling your livestock as well. When you have good connections to other homesteaders some breeds will be sold in the blink of an eye. As far as meat products go, animals such as heritage turkeys, ducks and geese all go for a high price in most markets, as does locally grown, grass fed beef. Alternatively, raising and selling tilapia or other fish in your local market is a massive money maker for many homesteaders.

When it comes to livestock, fiber animals are another great investment. Sheep and other animals that produce wool can be sheared often and their fibers can fetch a decent price in the local markets. You might be surprised to learn that you can make a fair amount of money selling worms or even slugs. Compose worms are easy to raise and quick to sell if there is a fishing community in your area. And slugs are a great delicacy in the French kitchen (but fishermen love them too, honestly). You could even consider selling other bugs as well. From grasshoppers to maggots, people will buy them for many purposes. Animal food is a great niche to get into when you want to get a little freaky with some slimy or crawly bugs. They are generally low maintenance and are more than willing to feed on the leftovers of your other crops.

Depending on the type of livestock you keep, a successful homestead entrepreneur should never discount the possibility of breeding. You can both rent out your studs to other homesteaders and farmers or find other homesteader who you can pay to breed additional livestock for you. This is a much cheaper option than purchasing additional, fully grown livestock and your profits double with every new animal you acquire. Great for scaling up your homesteading business efficiently!

Rabbits

Rabbits and bunnies are a popular commodity in most communities. This is partly because they breed like, well, rabbits. Check with your local zoning laws to see if you're able to sell baby rabbits to families in your community, because who doesn't want an adorable little bunny rabbit hopping around? If your bunny or rabbit won't sell as a pet, unfortunately for the rabbits, they will always sell very well as high-quality organically produced rabbit meat. This meat will sell either in your local farmer's market or, much more likely, to restaurants that serve them as rare delicacies.

Hunting

For those who own a lot of land that you use to hunt and forage, there is plenty of money to be made by leasing it out to hunters. Check your local zoning laws first to make sure that you have all of the necessary certification, then put an ad out in your local paper announcing that your hunting grounds are open for business. Hunting is only suitable if you own a lot of land that is not great for homesteading. An example can be a land that is required by the federal or state government to be nature, which allows you to use it for a limited number of purposes (and those purposes often do not include agriculture).

If you don't live on land that has the possibility of hunting for wild game, but you still have a decent amount of land to play with, consider opening a gun range and/or archery range. If you're handy with a bow and arrow, you could make a killing teaching archery classes to the community. See how easy it is do diversity and differentiate to income streams on your homestead? Your only limitation to making money is your own creativity.

Beekeeping

Beekeeping is a trade that many homestead entrepreneurs have taken to. That's because the markup on local, organic honey is huge and is always in demand. But primarily, it is a great natural and organic way to pollinate your crops and allow them to cross-breed using little to no effort. It will take a bit of an investment and relatively large startup cost, but after your first season, you should be able to recoup your entire initial investment and keep the profits buzzing. There are many hobbyists who are willing to rent a portion of your land to keep their bees for you, so feel free to put out some ads for beekeeping property as well. They provide a great service to your crops and are essential to any type of local biodiversity.

Tool Repair

Never forget to utilize every single resource in your utility belt. If you're pretty good at fixing, cleaning and sharpening your own homestead tools, you can charge other people to repair their tools as well. And in the process you will save a whole lot on tool maintenance for your own tools.

The same goes for gun maintenance for states that allow firearms. Gun owners truly love to take good care of their firearms, and if you are skilled with the mechanics of a gun and can perform simple repairs and modifications then there is definitely good money out there for you. You see a good combination here with the gun range we proposed earlier? I sure do: always combine your business ideas and allow multiple services to combine, get together and interact for maximum efficiency and customer satisfaction!

Similarly, people who use knives every day as part of their jobs, such as chefs, hairdressers and farmers, will pay a professional with a steady hand to have their instruments sharpened. It only takes a few minutes and you can charge anywhere from $20 to $100 per client. The initial investment of sharpening stones is rather small and the skill is not that hard to acquire, but nonetheless still difficult to master. Just give it a go and you will see how much appreciated such a service will be in the local community you're active in.

Use Every Inch!

When it comes to utilizing your indoor space, herbs and mushrooms should be a strong consideration. Orchards, berry bushes and vineyards can be grown along pretty much any walls surrounding your house, backyard or the perimeter of your property. Basically, you should be trying to utilize every inch of space at your disposal.

If your horizontal space is occupied by other activities, consider going into the great heights with vertical gardening solutions. These require some amount of investment, but will certainly allow you to get a good return on your investment quickly, because of all the space you free up by implementing these vertical spaces.

Homemade Items

Start thinking outside of the box and the let the homestead entrepreneur inside of you run free. Once you have dedicated customers or a booth at your local farmer's market, brainstorm ideas for other items that your customers will buy. Everyone loves fresh homemade French bread, buns, cinnamon rolls and hotcakes. Bring a hot batch of bread and pastries the next time you're vending your produce and people in the area will be unable to resist the smell. Similarly, homemade jams, jellies and preserves can be sold for a decent price in most markets. If you're growing plenty of different herbs, consider selling dried herbs and making tinctures. The markup on organic, local herbal blends and tinctures is incredible. Collaborate with your local bakery if necessary. It's more than worth it, believe me.

If you're committed to living off of the land, you'll want to take stock of all skills available to you and consider learning a few new trades as well. Pretty much any product that is locally grown and homemade bring in a fair amount of money, but as always, you want to consider the time it will take to learn a new skill and produce a sellable product before you jump into anything.

Items like homemade soaps, lotions, balms, candles and much more can also be sold at your local farmer's market. You could even easily sell them on an online platform such as Etsy. If you or anyone in your family has sewing skills, creating homemade hats, gloves, scarves, blankets and other linens is fun, easy and lucrative way to pass the time until your next harvest. If you have carpentry skills, you can create rustic style, hand crafted furniture or other wooden items, like small trinkets of children's toys. The same goes for metal working. Always have something to do when harvesting time is over and you cannot afford to scale up your business just yet. Think of any type of skill you have and allow yourself to take the time and make a little niche business out of those ideas as well. Truly, traditional hand-crafted products are always in demand and people will surely be more than willing to buy them from you in your own little homemade shop, or alternatively in your own farmer's webshop as well!

Just like the original homesteaders centuries ago, if you're going to live off of your land, be sure that nothing goes to waste. If you have any extra soil or firewood, both can also fetch a decent price in the market. Or alternatively, they might serve a great other use on your own land. Having a dedicated plot of land that you use to grave your livestock is a luxury in urbanized areas. You can charge other homesteaders to graze their livestock on your property. Even your livestock waste can be refined into the perfect fertilizer and sold at a decent price.

Daycare

Think about it – if you're at home all day anyway and your current batch of crops don't require 24/7 attention, you can make a killing watching after several neighborhood kids while you tend to your crops. You could even learn them a thing or two about farming in the process. Setting up a small daycare facility could be as simple as posting a few ads in your local newspaper, on Craigslist, or just by putting up fliers around town. Part-time daycare is a perfect way to earn extra income for homestead families who already have a couple of critters of their own crawling around.

Similarly, if you have a few pets of your own, or enjoy the company of dogs, there is decent money to be made with a doggie daycare service or even a more luxury pet hotel. As an added bonus, if you are skilled at training animals, pet owners will pay top dollar for obedience courses.

Hosting

Some more out-of-the-box ideas include renting out your house as a bed and breakfast to give your guests a first-hand taste of life on the homestead. In many places, there is a huge market for bed and breakfasts. If you live in a very picturesque location, you can make a killing by turning your backyard or barn into the ideal location to host weddings and other events on your property.

The same goes for photographers. Put an ad up with pictures of your homestead and let photographers in your area know that you are renting out your property for photo shoots. You can make an easy $100 per hour this way, or even more depending on the project you're attracting and the beauty of your homestead location.

Classes

Consider hosting classes on your homestead to teach the community your skills. Many successful homesteaders say that some of their most popular classes are cheese making, fiber arts, meat processing soap making, candle making in addition to giving tours. You can use popular smartphone or tablet apps such as for example: MeetUp, Coach.me or even Craigslist to announce and schedule different classes around the year.

Classes are a great way to give back some valuable experiences to the community, but you should also consider the added benefit in connecting with many types of locals that could become your next costumers. Always attempt to introduce the people your little class to what you do and the products you sell, and you will have made some great free advertisement for your business!

Seasonal options: Pumpkin Patch or Christmas Trees

Lastly, many homesteaders early anticipate Halloween season when they turn their homestead into a pumpkin patch and open it up to the public. Children love to pick out their own favorite pumpkins for their Halloween festivities, and it is a great opportunity to network and introduce people to your other products as well. Not only is this a great idea to sell pumpkins, but it is great fun and even local news publicity, too!

This is also very true for Christmas season, were Christmas trees are perpetually in high demand. These trees take little to no upkeep and allow for a good extra income. And when you think outside of the box a little more, you can allow people from the local community to adopt their own Christmas trees and teach them to take care of their tree themselves. This way your homestead will get known locally very quickly and you will be able to build up a network of willing customers that take interest in your products.

On that note, becoming a facet of the community will be your greatest ally when it comes time to start your business. Getting exposure in your local farmer's market is one thing, but calling your local newspapers and making headlines is one of the best things you can do for your homestead. We'll cover much more on the subject of getting publicity and marketing the products you grow in your homestead later in this book. As you can see, there are plenty of inventive ways in which homesteader in this day and age can make a living and have great fun while doing it!

Starting Your Business

Now that you have a basic idea of all of the ways you can turn your land into dollar signs, you're probably excited to start your own homestead business. In this section, we'll go over how to get your business license and what type of certifications you may require in order to make your homestead business as successful as it can possibly be. Please note that it is very difficult to pinpoint the exact procedure for all regions and that these procedures can and will be different depending on where you live.

In the United States, every state varies in terms of the documents you need to file and the fees you are required to pay when it comes to obtaining a business license for your homestead. At the very least, you will be required to fill out an Articles of Organization form and mail it to your Secretary of State's office along with a small fee. All of the documents you need in order to make your homestead a government recognized business are available for free at your state's business division website.

If your gross income is over $20,000, you will need to file for a Homestead Food license in most states. This is as simple as going to your states Department of Agriculture website and applying for a license online. You will be asked to provide a few tax documents, answer some questions about your homestead and pay a small fee before you receive your official Homestead Food license.

Again, we must emphasize here that the regulations and requirements for every state are different. Be sure to check your states requirements before starting your homestead business or selling produce (especially meat and dairy products) to the general public. And if you're outside of the U.S., please consult your local Ministry of Agriculture or business advisor. If needed, ask a legal advisor about the things you're allowed to do and the things you should certainly try to avoid if you don't want to be in trouble.

Acquiring customers

Your first and best customers will be restaurants in your area. You'll find that selling your crops business to business is much easier than selling them individually in the market, especially if you can get a restaurant to commit to consistent a weekly or monthly order.

Start by going to all of the restaurants within 5 miles of your homestead and asking to speak with the manager. If you can't speak with the manager, ask to speak with the head chef. The best places to go are mom-and-pop shops rather than franchise restaurants who usually cannot deviate from the food ordering system that their company has laid out for them. The best time to go to a restaurant is when they are slowest, such as Monday through Thursday, either when they first open up or just after their lunch rush. This will ensure that the manager has your undivided attention.

Explain to the manager or head chef what you do and what you can offer them. If they express any interest, offer to bring some samples by for them to try out. Even more efficient is to already bring some of your best samples in yourself. If they are not interested in the crops you grow, ask them what ingredients they would be willing to purchase that is grown locally and organically from your homestead. It's important to never discuss specific prices on your first meeting with a restaurant. This can always be negotiated later.

If you and the restaurant cannot come to an agreement, kindly invite them to come out to the next farmer's market even that you're vending to try out some of our fresh produce. After you've visited all of the restaurants within 5 miles from your homestead, if you still haven't reached your maximum capacity by selling all of the crops when they're ready to harvest, try going to all of the restaurants within 10 miles, and so forth. You'll find that the further you get from your homestead, the less likely restaurants will be to buy your crops. A good rule of thumb is don't sell to anyone that is further than you would like to drive.

If you make any of the homemade items we mentioned in the last section, such as soaps, lotions, candles, etc., try going into your local mom-and-pop convenience stores and ask them the same thing. If they are unwilling to buy a whole case of your homemade products to sell in their store, ask if you can display them somewhere in their store. Let the store owner know that you will kindly give them a percent of each item that sells – that's basically free money for store owners! Go back the each week to take inventory and collect your sales, minus the store owners' small commission.

In addition to selling to local restaurants and merchants, you will want to look into selling at your local farmer's market. Unless the regular orders that the restaurants in your area are keeping you busy to maximum capacity, the products you sell at your farmer's market will be your second best source of income.

Check with your city to see where and when farmer's markets are held. Because the vendors at farmer's markets are doing the community a service, the city usually won't charge an arm and a leg for a booth. In fact, most cities will provide you with your own table and canopy. It's up to you to present your products in the best way possible. If you plan on becoming a facet at your local farmer's market, definitely consider investing in a canvas banner (about the same size as the table the city provides you with), business cards that list the products you sell as well as other fun items to give away to potential customers, such as stickers, free samples or candy for the kids.

Learning and diversifying from the competition

Take a look at what other successful vendors at your local farmer's market are doing. How do they display their products? What are they selling? How do they interact with customers? By scoping out the competition ahead of time, you'll get a better idea if setting up a booth at your local farmer's market is the right decision for you. Obviously, if you're main crop is mushroom and there are three other mushroom vendors at the farmer's market, you should probably wait until you have something new and interesting to sell before getting a booth.

If your city does not have an existing farmer's market, you can organize one yourself fairly easily by calling around to other local growers, homesteaders and farmers and asking if they are interested in participating in a farmer's market. Once you have at least 8 other vendors on board, contact your city and let them know your plan. Suggest several different locations that you think would make a great farmer's market – one that is easily accessible by people – and make sure that the local newspaper prints ads at least a month beforehand. The city will almost always have a ton of paperwork for you to fill out, and chance are the city council will have the talk it over, but ultimately, you should be able to get a farmer's market going in your city in just a month or two.

Another place you will want to set up shop is your very own home. Depending on how accessible your homestead is to the public, consider building a little booth or storefront on your porch or front lawn to sell items to the public – much like you would at the farmer's market.

You can also make a killing selling your homemade items in online stores like Etsy and eBay. You'll need to set up an account for your store on either site, create an attractive store description that tells the story of your homestead as well as a logo for your store.

The key to selling these items online is to write a captivating product description. Describe the item you're selling as well as what it's made from and a little bit about the process of making it. It's also important to take a good picture of the product that you're selling. Look at the product photos that other online stores who sell homemade goods are using for inspiration. You'll want to take a close-up picture of your product with a solid, white background for the best effect. List the price of your item close to the price of similar homemade items from other online stores. Over time, you'll find that your online store can generate a much larger income than that of your farmer's market sales. Of course, the only way that you'll sell your homestead products is to make sure that the people who want to buy them know about them.

Marketing on the Homestead

What are the best ways to get the word out that the products grown on your homestead are the finest in the land? In this section, we'll go over some of the best ways to help you market, promote and sell all of the crops that your produce on your homestead.

Restaurants

When you're trying to attract more local restaurants, the first thing that you should have already done by now is to touch base with all of your local restaurants and let them know about your business and what fresh, organic and locally grown crops you can offer them. Understand the needs of each individual restaurant in your area, what produce they usually use and what they are interested in buying from you, even if they're not currently customers. Keep track of every restaurant you visit and meet the manager or head chef, when you visited them and what their specific needs are in terms of ordering produce. Even if they aren't yet ready to order from you, don't give up just yet. Every restaurant needs fresh and locally grown produce, so if they simply need something that you don't currently grow, be sure and write that down so that you can consider growing that crop in the future.

If you ever have a restaurant suddenly stop a regular order of your crops because they recently changed their menu, you'll have a whole list of other local restaurants prepared to sell to. Keeping track of what types of crops that restaurants are willing to buy is also helpful when rotating crops for different seasons. That way, no matter what crop is in season, you'll have a cash crop prepared and ready to be sold to any number of local restaurants.

Especially important when just starting your homestead, be sure and bring a fresh crop of free samples to restaurants who may become future customers. Make sure that the restaurant managers or head chefs know the benefits of buying locally sourced, organic produce. While most restaurants already know the massive benefits to buying from homesteads instead of importing their food, be sure to reaffirm this with them. You may also want to consider giving new restaurant customers a one-time discount for placing a new order from you. If you ever have new types of crops to offer, you can easily persuade restaurants into placing weekly orders if that is an ingredient that they already use and you are offering it to them at a discounted price.

Local Markets

Once you've become a facet at your local farmer's market, it will be easier to attract more and more customers simply by word of mouth, but successful homestead entrepreneurs don't simply rely on referrals to make their money. Instead of simply asking your customers to tell their friends about you, offer them an incentive. For example, you could make coupons for people who bring in new customers to your booth for 50% off of bother of their purchase. This will ensure that you are consistently bringing in new customers, and the discounted 50% off of one purchase is essentially negligible when you consider the long term revenue that a life-long customer will bring in.

There are many things that you can do to promote your vending booth at the local farmer's market, starting with simple things such as posting fliers around town advertising your homestead and the items you sell at the market. A good place to hang these is at the area where the farmer's market takes place on the days of the week when there are no events. Any highly trafficked place in your city is a great opportunity to promote your famer's market booth.

Taking out ads in your local newspaper is another great way to promote your booth at the local market. These ads are relatively inexpensive when you ask to purchase ad space over the course of several months. Spend a little extra to get a nice-looking graphic advertisement as opposed to an all text ad. Images are so much more effective at catching reader's eyes than an all text ads, which they are highly likely to simply skim over. 4" by 4", or even 2" by 4" is a good advertisement size to start with. This will make sure that people reading the newspaper will see your ad. Your ads should feature the name of your business or homestead, a few images of graphics, where customers can find you at the farmer's market and what products you offer. Be sure to emphasis the quality and freshness of your organic and locally grown produce, which is the main appeal of such items at a farmer's market.

Don't forget to ask your customers who purchase form your booth at the farmer's market where they heard about you. While most will say they just saw your booth and walked right up, this is the only way to gauge how effective your advertisements are. Keep track of the number of people who tell you that they saw your ad in the local newspaper. If a few weeks go by and you still haven't had anyone tell you that they saw your ad, it might be time to pull it out of the paper. Basically, any way that you can reach your potential customers will bring you one step closer to your next sale and additional profit potential from your homesteading operation.

During any event where you are vending your items, make sure to have a variety of free marketing materials to give away to prospective customers, including business cards, free samples and even treats for the kids. Giving away candy that you make yourself is a great way to attract customers. When children come up to your booth and ask if they can take a piece of candy, which is a perfect opportunity to strike up a conversation with their parents and show them everything that you have for sell.

Online Stores

For all of those homemade items that you sell online, you could spend a lifetime marketing those in different ways. Since running your homestead is your top priority, we'll briefly cover some of the most effective ways to help you sell your homemade items online.

Earlier in this book, we briefly talked about the best way to create a listing for one of your homemade products when selling them at online stores such as eBay or Etsy. It's also important for modern homestead entrepreneurs to have their own website. You can pay someone a couple of hundred dollars to create a gorgeous looking homestead website for you, complete with your own e-commerce online store, or in the interest of being self-sufficient, you can create your own.

Start by buying a domain name and hosting from a popular web hosting service. These can be obtained for as little as $12. You can build your own website with WordPress and an online store using a downloadable plugin called WooCommerce for free.

Selling your own homemade products right from their own website is one of the biggest ways that successful homestead entrepreneurs are able to make so much money.

If you produce a large quantity of different homemade items that you sell both locally and online, then consider hiring someone to take over all aspects of marketing and promotion of your online store. This will free up a lot of your own time as your sales for these online stores go through the roof now that you have a dedicated professional working on them full-time. If revenue from your online product sales are one of your best sources of income, then you may want to consider stocking up on your best-sellers, then sending all of your homemade items to a distribution warehouse where they will be automatically shipped out anytime someone places an order from your online store. This will save you the headache of packaging and shipping everything out yourself. Whenever you can find a way to save yourself time by automating any part of your homestead, grab on to it. Second only to information, time is one of your most precious resources on the homestead.

Whether you sell online or not, a huge part of running a successful business in this day and age is customer service and connecting with your customers in an authentic way. This is why all successful businesses today, as well as homestead entrepreneurs, have a presence on social media. Social media marketing for small businesses can drive massive amounts of customers to your online store. Create accounts for your homestead on all of the prominent social networks such as Facebook, Twitter, Instagram, Pinterest, Google Plus, Reddit and anywhere else you think you might find new customers. Don't forget to create a LinkedIn page as well so that you can network with other homestead entrepreneurs and restaurant owners. Start by letting your customer and other people in your area know that you're on social media. You can even offer exclusive discount codes online to new customers.

Once you have a presence online, attracting new customer is as easy as posting pictures of your latest crops. Let your followers online get a glimpse of your homestead through social media. When people feel engaged by your photos and your personal story, they will be much more likely to buy from you. This also goes for customers who visit your local market vending booth and don't need a "sale's pitch" in order to buy your crops, because you've already built up a relationship with them over social media.

The key to successful social media marketing and finding new customers is to post on all of your social networks frequently. You need to build up a relationship with your customers online just as you would build a relationship with your customers at the local farmer's market.

You should also consider using pay-per-click advertisements, such as Google AdWords of Facebook Ads, as a way of getting your products in front of the right target audience. You don't need a massive advertising budget to help you sell more of your homestead products online; just a few ads to target the people in your area or who have an interest in buying homemade products similar to the ones you provide.

Homestead Storefront

Lastly, never forget about selling your crops to people who visit your homestead. There is nothing better than customers coming to you to buy your crops, and people in the community love to get their crops straight from the source when they are at their freshest. Attracting attention to your in-house sales is not so different that selling your crops at the local farmer's market. Most of your customers will come from people you've met at other events where you're vending your crops, which is why it's important to always let people know that you also sell these same items at their utmost freshest right from your homestead. Having your address right on your business card will make this process much easier, as well as providing discounts for walk-up customers and customer referrals.

Another great way of attracting walk-up customers to your homestead storefront is to post signs or fliers around the streets in your neighborhood with directions to your homestead as well as the types of products you carry. Simple signs that say things like "Homemade Jams & Jellies This Way", along with direction arrows, could drive massive amounts of local traffic to your homestead storefront depending on where you're located.

Being a successful homestead entrepreneur doesn't stop once you harvest your last crop of the season. Making the sale is one of the most important aspects of homesteading. Follow the tips outlined above and you'll soon have every cash crop that you produce sold before it even leaves the ground.

The Homesteader Do's & Don'ts

In this section you will learn some of the lesser known tips and tricks related to homesteading. We'll show you some of the secrets that successful homestead entrepreneurs are doing to keep everything running just the way it's supposed to while keeping the cash flowing. We'll also show you some common mistakes made by first time homesteaders and how you can avoid them.

Never get so caught up in your cash crops that you lose track of maintaining your homestead. It's important that you develop regular maintenance habits early on. Check all of the tools that you use at least once a week for rust or damage. Can you really afford to run out and buy another expensive tool in the middle of the week? Similarly, if you keep livestock, be mindful of their health at all times. If you see that one of your animals is sick or acting strange, call your local vet before it's too late.

Have a contingency plan for everything. Just as you did while planning your homestead, so should you plan every aspect of your business? Have both a short-term and long-term goal in mind for your homestead as well as for each individual cash crop. Always crunch the numbers and do your math before jumping into a new investment. Never neglect balancing your books and itemizing your finances after a sale. If you're not good with balancing books, find someone who is, or hire someone.

On that note, have a team. It doesn't matter what business you're in, no one person can manage all aspects of a successful business. If you are working with your family exclusive, make sure that everyone knows exactly what their jobs are and that they have the skills and knowledge to perform them properly. If you're particularly good at once aspect of running a homestead, focus all of your energy on that have hire people to do all of the other work.

Running a homestead requires an abundance of skills. Take an honest inventory of what you're good at and learn a few handy new skills. Whenever you can find the time, try to teach yourself a new skill or ability that you can apply to your homestead. You'll find that it's easy to cut costs here and there by doing more things by yourself. At the same time, never be afraid to hire someone to take on a task that you're just not suited for.

One of the first things that every homestead should know is how to use every tool in his or her toolbox. Invest in a good set of tools that are durable. Anything that offers a lifetime warranty is a good bet.

In the spirit of being self-sufficient, you should always be looking for new ways to reuse items around your house, especially things which may otherwise go to waste. For example, earlier in this book, we talked briefly about refining and selling the waste of your livestock as fertilizer, which could also be used in your own garden and for crops.

Another upgrade to your homestead you may want to consider is adding a renewable energy source. Investing in solar panels, wind turbines or a hydropower system may have a high initial startup cost, but will save you money in the long run. Instead of using a traditional heater to heat your home in the winter, simply cut firewood and burn it in a stove or fireplace. Also consider switching to alternative fuel sources, such as biomass, ethanol or biodiesel. All of these small changes could save you thousands of dollars over a ten year period.

Another great upgrade to your homestead that is shared by a majority of successful homestead entrepreneurs? Dogs. Every good homestead, especially those that are far out in rural areas, should have a dog to guard your crops, livestock and your family.

By now, you probably have all of your best-selling cash crops figured out. Now take another look at your shopping list – what items on their can be grown in your own homestead? Calculate the cost of the items you want to discontinue permanently from your shopping list, look up the average time that it would take to grow them and find out how much room they would take up in your homestead. If you're homestead is already overflowing with cash crops, it might be wiser to simply buy everything at the grocery store, but if you have the room to grow these items for you and your family then you can enjoy your own fresh fruits and vegetables for the investment of only a few seeds.

On a similar note, if you're planting crops in large amounts, you will need to rotate them every season so that you don't completely deplete the soil of all of its rich nutrients. This sounds like a basic requirement and something every farmer knows, but you would be surprised how often this is forgotten in practice.

The secret to becoming a successful homestead entrepreneur is to practice the "better safe than sorry" philosophy. When you're able to keep everything in your homestead balanced, you'll find that life on the homestead runs smoothly. When you reached most of your basic objectives towards your homesteading business, it is time to consider if you want to expand further. Are you willing to make more investments in order to increase your influence and profits? Let us overthink some essential business expansion tips and techniques as a closing note to our homestead introduction.

Expanding Your Business

Of course, every good homesteader will eventually face the same predicament: you want to expand your homestead business, but there is just not enough room! How do we scale up the homesteading business with the limitations that our lands bring?

In this section, we'll share some tips and techniques you can use when it comes time to grow your urban farming operation. For any type of business, it is the art of outsourcing that allows you to increase your revenue and business scope. Nobody is able to juggle all the activities outlined in this book at the same time. You will be required to hire some experienced and skillful people when you're looking to expand drastically, and that includes having to pay for their services.

Outsourcing is a topic I could write a whole other book about, but there are plenty of resources out there that will teach you the basics of becoming a successful people's manager and learn others about your profession. The key takeaway for now should be:

do not be afraid to let some tasks be taken over by other people, even if you yourself are more skillful and experienced at those tasks. As a business owner, you simply do not have the time to juggle between all your tasks. Always hire people to do simple work for them, and allow yourself to delegate some of your own tasks to them.

If your homesteading business is doing well, the most common solution is to purchase more land. Depending on what your biggest cash crop is, look for a piece of land that can accommodate as much of that crops as possible. A quick online search will give you an idea of what properties are available in your area.

If you plan on managing your new property yourself, you'll want to find one that is as close to your home as possible to minimize commute. Alternatively, you can find a property that is closer to one of your big clients and hire someone to manage it for you.

If you haven't already, hiring people to work for you is one of the most rewarding parts of being a homestead entrepreneur. You get to contribute to the welfare of other people in your community in addition to contributing to their overall health with your delicious, locally grown food. When looking for employees, do yourself a favor and pay a little extra to find someone with a history of experience in the task you plan to have them do. Taking the time to train someone with no experiencing in agriculture is a recipe for disaster. When you pay for minimum wage labor, you get minimum wage work, which may end up causing your more headaches than dollars. Running a homestead is difficult enough, and the last thing you want to worry about is an employee who doesn't know how to do their job.

Always remember to crunch your numbers and balance your books before taking on any new investments, especially large scale purchases. Investing in another property is a huge step for a homesteader.

Parting Words

Living and working on a homestead is a never ending job. There is always room for improvement and always more to grow. This is as much an occupational journey as it is a personal one. Becoming a homestead entrepreneur will allow you to learn and grow as a person as you watch your business grow. Like most things in life, it won't always be an easy journey, but the benefits and happiness resulting from working on your personal piece of land are also limitless.

While managing your own homestead, you'll be able to provide for your family in a self-sufficient way. Being self-sufficient is a hard-earned reward in and of itself. You'll also enjoy the benefits of food security that are not available to many people.

Thank you for reading *Homesteading For Beginners*. Through the course of this book, we have showed you how to properly plan out your own homestead, how to budget for every aspect of your homestead, tips and tricks used by some of the most successful homestead entrepreneurs, some of the best cash crops available to homestead entrepreneurs, how and where you can sell them, different ways in which you can market the products made on your homestead, how to expand your business when that time comes and we have brought you one step closer to complete self-sufficiency.

If this book was helpful to you or if you enjoyed reading this book, please consider leaving an honest review. This allows other readers to make an informed decision on purchasing this book. It also helps me with the visibility of this book. An honest review is therefore greatly appreciated. Please refer to the page you bought this book to leave your review, or consult the e-mail you will receive several hours after your purchase. Thank you for your consideration.

- William Walsworth